NINA RAINE

Nina Raine's other plays include *Tiger Country* (Hampstead, London, 2011); *Tribes* (Royal Court, London, 2010) and an adaptation of *The Drunks* by the Durnenkov Brothers (Royal Shakespeare Company, 2009). She was shortlisted for the 2004 Verity Bargate Award and awarded the 2006 Evening Standard and Critics' Circle Awards for Most Promising Playwright for her debut play *Rabbit*.

Her work as a director includes *Tiger Country* (Hampstead, London); *Unprotected* (Liverpool Everyman/Traverse, Edinburgh); *Rabbit* (Old Red Lion Theatre/Trafalgar Studios/59East59 Theatre, New York); *Vermillion Dream* (Salisbury Playhouse); *Eskimo Sisters* (Southwark, London) and *Shades* (Royal Court, London). Awards include the 2006 Best Director TMA Award and the 2006 Amnesty International Freedom of Expression Award.

Other Titles in this Series

Nina Raine

RABBIT

NICK HERN BOOKS

London

www.nickhernbooks.co.uk

A Nick Hern Book

Rabbit first published in Great Britain as a paperback original in 2006 by
Nick Hern Books, The Glasshouse, 49a Goldhawk Road, London W12 8QP

Reprinted with revisions in 2007, 2009, 2011 (twice), 2012

Rabbit copyright © 2006 Nina Raine

Nina Raine has asserted her right to be identified as the author of this work

Cover image: Eureka! Design Consultants Ltd
Cover design: Ned Hoste, 2H

Typeset by Country Setting, Kingsdown, Kent CT14 8ES
Printed in the UK by Mimeo Ltd, Huntingdon, Cambridgeshire PE29 6XX

A CIP catalogue record for this book is available from the British Library

ISBN   978 1 85459 935 3

Woodland
CARBON
www.woodlandcarbon.co.uk
NICK HERN BOOKS
Printed on Carbon Captured paper

Rabbit was first performed at the Old Red Lion Theatre, London, on 16 May 2006. The production transferred to the Trafalgar Studios, West End, on 5 September 2006. The cast was as follows:

BELLA	Charlotte Randle
FATHER	Hilton McRae
EMILY	Ruth Everett
TOM	Rocky Marshall
RICHARD	Adam James
SANDY	Susannah Wise

Director	Nina Raine
Designer	Jaimie Todd
Lighting Designer	Colin Grenfell
Sound Designer	Fergus O'Hare

To my parents

Characters

BELLA, *late twenties*

FATHER, *late fifties*

EMILY, *late twenties*

TOM, *late twenties/early thirties. Possibly black, or, if white, more London/street than the others.*

RICHARD, *early thirties. R.P.*

SANDY, *late twenties/early thirties. Amazonian. Accent could be either London or elsewhere.*

The girls are all attractive, but should be different 'types' physically – hair colour, height, etc. Ditto the men.

The main setting is the restaurant and the table at which the friends sit. But the area lit should be small and intimate: and it is in the darkness around this focal point that the father's scenes materialise.

Author's note about the angel chimes: in my experience, relying on the heat of the candles to turn the angels naturally is not ideal, since a theatre's air conditioning and the body heat of the audience significantly affect air-flow and interfere with the turning of the chimes. Therefore, it is probably preferable for the chimes to be a prop, made with real candles and a battery pack in the base that will turn the angels no matter what.

ACT ONE

BELLA*'s* FATHER *sitting on a sofa in a dressing gown.*
BELLA *standing. They are looking at a little wooden table.*

BELLA. No.

Beat.

No.

FATHER. No?

BELLA. No.

FATHER. You can't see it?

BELLA. I can't see it.

FATHER. Look at it.

Beat.

Go over there. Go over there and look at it.

BELLA. Dad –

FATHER. Go over there and look at it. Take a proper look at it.
Touch it.

BELLA *goes over to the little table. She runs her hand
over it.*

BELLA. It's a table. Wood. There's nothing there.

FATHER. No, look at it.

BELLA. I *am* looking at it.

FATHER. Look at it properly.

Pause.

There's a pattern on it. Just over the top there. A pattern all
over it. These . . . dots.

Beat.

Over the top of it.

Beat.

See it now?

Lots of red and gold –

Red and gold –

Clicks fingers.

Red and gold –

BELLA (*one hand on the table*). Spots?

Shakes his head.

Circles?

Shakes his head.

FATHER. Red and gold. (*Clicks fingers again.*)

Red and gold. (*He makes a diamond shape with his hands.*)

BELLA (*comes slowly back to sit down*). Diamonds.

FATHER. Red and gold diamonds all over it. Beautiful.

BELLA. You just need to practise. The words come back.

FATHER. But you can see it.

Beat.

BELLA. No.

FATHER. You said diamonds.

BELLA. I guessed.

Beat.

You can get the words back. The words come back. The words –

FATHER. Stop talking to me about the words. I don't want to talk about the fucking words. It –

BELLA. Oh for Christ's sake, Dad. The words. The pattern. It's the same thing.

FATHER. No.

BELLA. Dad, it is. Don't let's argue about this. Jesus. Ask anyone. The nurse –

FATHER. The nurse is wrong.

BELLA. That's why your words –

FATHER. The words, the words, the words. I know. You said. You said. She said.

He makes a sweeping gesture with his hand.

The words – (*Again.*)

The words are a – (*Again.*)

The words are a –

Finally.

' . . . passing thing.'

Beat.

BELLA. They can be recovered.

FATHER. They can't be recovered.

Silence.

BELLA. Dad –

FATHER. Listen.

Just listen a moment.

Pause.

Can you hear that?

Pause.

Can you hear that? You must be able to hear that.

They are both quiet. The buzzing of a fly.

BELLA. A fly.

FATHER. Well, thank Christ we agree about *something*.

Beat. They listen. It stops.

Listen. Let me tell you something. I'm going to be fine.

Silence. They look at each other. The fly starts to buzz again. Blackout. The buzzing of the fly turns into the buzzing of –

A restaurant. Two girls sit in the bar area, at a low table. EMILY and BELLA. EMILY is looking over BELLA's shoulder. BELLA waits in a state of tension.

A pause.

EMILY (*decisively*). No.

BELLA (*overlapping*). Keep your *voice* down!

EMILY (*a whisper*). Al*right*!

> *Beat. A hoarse stage whisper.*

> I said, 'No.'

BELLA (*hoarse whisper*). He hasn't seen me?

EMILY. He hasn't seen you.

> *They wait. A tense pause.*

> It's fine. He's not even looking over here. He's going over to the bar. He's right over there.

BELLA. You sure he didn't see me?

EMILY. He's at the bar.

BELLA. Did he see me?

EMILY. He's getting two drinks.

BELLA. OK.

EMILY. It's OK. He didn't see you.

BELLA. OK.

> *They both relax.*

EMILY. So who is he?

BELLA. He's 'Tom'.

EMILY. Yeah 'Tom', you said, but which 'Tom'?

BELLA. You know which Tom. You know. I mean, how many Toms are there! Don't make me feel like a slut!

EMILY. But you are a slut.

BELLA. There's only one Tom. I treated him like shit. That Tom.

EMILY. Oh. (*Looks.*)

BELLA. Yeah.

> *Beat.*

EMILY. He's coming back.

BELLA. Shit.

EMILY. He's coming back this way.

BELLA. Shit. Can he see us?

EMILY follows TOM's movements.

EMILY. Wait a sec. No. He's going to a table . . . Two girls
sitting at it . . .

He's sitting down . . . He's facing the girls . . . You're OK.
He hasn't seen us.

Beat.

BELLA. He *must* have seen us! How can he go right up to the
bar and back again and not see us?

EMILY. Because he wasn't looking over here.

BELLA. What the fuck does he think he's playing at? If he
comes past here again I'm going to say something to him.

EMILY. I thought you didn't want to see him!

BELLA. Yes, but he's ignoring me. He's *ignoring* me.

Fuck that, I'm going to go over there *now* and get him.

EMILY. *Get* him?

BELLA. Yeah.

Small beat.

EMILY. You're a bully when you're drunk, d'you know that?

BELLA. That's what my mum always says.

EMILY. What do you mean, '*get* him'?

BELLA. Get him and bring him over here. I want to show him
to you. You can have a proper look at him.

EMILY. I don't *want* a proper look at him.

BELLA. You'll like him.

EMILY. I won't like him.

BELLA. Back in a sec.

EMILY. Bella, don't. (BELLA *is going*.) For Christ's sake . . .
(BELLA *is gone. To herself*.) Fantastic.

Beat. EMILY *drinks*. BELLA *returns with* TOM, *leading
him by the hand*.

TOM. Hi!

EMILY. Hi!

BELLA. This is Emily . . . Emily, this is Tom . . .

TOM. So, hi . . .

EMILY. Hi Tom . . . lovely to meet you . . .

BELLA. Sit down.

EMILY. Sorry, let me move my . . .

TOM. Sorry, don't let me . . .

EMILY. It's fine, it's fine . . .

BELLA. So, yeah! God, it's great to see you! I didn't know you came here . . .

TOM. I haven't seen you for . . . well, the last time was . . . How long have you been here, anyway?

BELLA. Why, do I look pissed? Did you know it's my birthday today?

TOM. Really? Shit! So . . . you're . . . you're a Scorpio?

BELLA. Sagittarius.

TOM. Sagittarius, of course.

Beat.

What are you two drinking? Let me get another bottle.

BELLA. No, no, we've got plenty here.

TOM (*holds bottle up to light*). It's nearly empty.

EMILY. So it is.

BELLA. Shit, that went fast.

Well, there are only two glasses of wine in a bottle, really.

EMILY. Let me get it, you two talk.

TOM. No, seriously, let me.

BELLA. Oh . . . Tom . . . are you sure?

TOM. I'll be two minutes.

BELLA. That's so sweet of you.

The second he has gone:

You know, he had one of those really thick cocks? I mean really thick. I'd never had one like it before.

EMILY (*interested despite herself*). Thick rather than long?

BELLA. Yeah. Really thick – not particularly long. But not uniformly thick – you know – like a traffic cone.

EMILY. Thicker at the bottom than at the tip, you mean?

BELLA (*gestures*). A Cornetto cock.

EMILY. I don't like them.

BELLA. Yeah. It did look scary. I remember.

EMILY. How thick?

BELLA. God, like about –

She starts to show with thumb and forefinger.

No, hang on – more like –

TOM *comes back. She turns to him, unflustered.*

No, wait, kind of – the base was – hi, did you –

TOM. Bella, I'm going to get red instead, is that OK?

BELLA. Sure! Get whatever looks good.

TOM. OK.

BELLA *barely waits for him to turn and go before carrying on.*

BELLA. Yeah, like *this*, I'd say.

EMILY. And the length?

BELLA. Umm . . . Sort of . . . .

Measures.

Maybe?

EMILY. Not so long then.

BELLA. No. But he had these gorgeous balls, I shaved them one time.

EMILY. Really? He let you?

BELLA. He found it a turn-on.

Beat.

Actually, come to think of it, we *did* have a good time

together. In bed. He was nice . . . Nothing in common though.

EMILY. Weren't you worried you might cut him? Shaving the balls?

BELLA. No. You know what I'm like, I'm very good with my hands, I'm good at all that stuff, threading needles, getting splinters out, fiddly stuff. Just don't use too much shaving cream and it's easy.

EMILY. And what was it like?

BELLA. Oh my God . . .

With one hand she fondles imaginary balls in the air, her eyes half-closed. TOM *returns, sits down.*

It made them feel so *soft* . . .

Hi, thanks. Great.

TOM (*putting down bottle*). Here we go . . .

EMILY (*looks at him appraisingly*). Thanks.

TOM (*handing out glasses*). Emily? Emily . . . Bella . . . and me.

Listen. I'm just going to – you get started on this without me. I'm just going to go over there and tell them – I'll be back in a second.

BELLA (*warmly*). It's great to see you, Tom.

He goes.

You know Lisa *still* hasn't spoken to me. Ever since she found out about me and (*Gestures.*) him.

EMILY. She found out? How did she find out?

BELLA. She asked me. Straight out. Whether anything happened – between me and him.

EMILY. Shit.

BELLA. So I told her the truth.

Beat.

EMILY. Why?

BELLA. She was asking me straight out. I couldn't lie, could I?

Beat.

EMILY. So what did you say?

BELLA. I told her. That we'd snogged each other.

EMILY. You'd snogged each other? You told her that you and Tom –

BELLA. Yes. I had to tell her the truth.

EMILY. But you didn't!

BELLA. Didn't what?

EMILY. Tell her the truth. You fucked him, Bella. You *fucked* him. Many times. You didn't just snog him.

BELLA. Oh right. Yeah.

Pause.

Well, I couldn't tell her *that*, could I? Obviously.

Anyway it doesn't matter. They'd broken up, anyway.

BELLA*'s phone rings. To phone:*

I don't know who you are.

'Mute.'

She mutes it.

May as well finish the old one.

She pours, emptying the bottle.

Twenty-nine.

EMILY. Twenty-nine.

They chink glasses.

BELLA. To me.

EMILY. To you.

They drink.

Who's actually *invited*?

BELLA. Oh, people. Nobody knows each other.

EMILY. Nobody I know?

BELLA. No. Men. Women. It's going to be a nightmare.

I decided I'd let all my friends meet each other.

EMILY. Why?

BELLA. I don't know.

You know I woke up this morning.

Six in the morning. I rolled over. One of my earplugs fell out. Like sleeping on a pebble. I woke up. I sat up. Inhaled a *frond* of snot – my nose is so blocked at the moment –

EMILY. – Poor you –

BELLA. – Went into the bathroom. Looked in the mirror. And squeezed a whitehead on my *neck*. And plucked a hair out of my nipple.

EMILY. Happy birthday.

They down their wine.

BELLA. Talk to me. Tell me about work.

EMILY. OK. Work.

Beat.

Well, work, I don't know, what can I say.

I just hate the fucking women.

BELLA. Yeah.

EMILY. The women are the worst.

BELLA. Course they're the worst.

EMILY. I don't mind the men. Well, the men aren't great but the women . . .

BELLA. I know. Don't tell me.

EMILY. There's this one doctor, right.

BELLA. Don't tell me.

EMILY. This fucking little careerist. Doctor Goulding. I haven't told you.

BELLA. So tell me.

EMILY. I have to shadow her. Before I qualify. They warned me she was difficult. Full of attitude. Unpleasant. But there's nothing I can do.

BELLA. Ask to change.

EMILY. I can't. Even though she's a cow.

BELLA. Why not?

EMILY. I'll be accused of discriminating.

BELLA. Discriminating against what?

EMILY. Well, a) she's a woman –

BELLA. *Yeah?* – So are you –

EMILY. And b) she's deaf.

BELLA. She's *deaf*?

EMILY. Stone deaf.

BELLA. A deaf doctor?

EMILY. So obviously I can't ask to be transferred. It would look so bad . . . – I know, a deaf doctor, can you imagine? I mean – you should see her stethoscope. She has to have this special one . . . it's like this huge . . . (*Gestures with hands*.) ' . . . '

BELLA. Thing.

EMILY. Exactly. And half the time I can't understand what she's asking me to do because, you know, she 'thntalks thnlike hnthis' . . .

BELLA. Oh no.

EMILY. So she gets impatient with me . . . And she's fucking *pushy*.

BELLA. Deaf and ambitious.

EMILY. And she's a complete man-eater. Pressed Alex up against the wall one day. Stuck her hand down his trousers. Can you imagine. He didn't know what to do. Didn't want to look . . . prejudiced. He couldn't tell anyone.

BELLA. Christ.

EMILY. I know.

BELLA. Sounds like a nightmare.

EMILY. And I wouldn't care. I wouldn't give a fuck. I mean, it's only three more weeks. But then someone told me – she's going to be made a registrar.

BELLA. Promotion?

EMILY. I mean – Registrar? She's my age! It's unheard of! And not only is she fucking *deaf* for a start, more importantly, she's a crap doctor!

BELLA. 'Young, Gifted and Deaf . . . '

EMILY. Bella –

BELLA. (Yeah yeah.)

EMILY. – This is serious.

BELLA. You'll get promoted.

EMILY. Can you see how depressing this is? She's *talentless*.

BELLA. Look. Emily.

EMILY. I know, I know, 'Poor thing', 'She's deaf' –

BELLA. Emily. Listen to me.

EMILY. – But that is going to open all sorts of doors for her!

BELLA. Listen to me. Emily. Let me tell you something. Stop – looking over your shoulder.

EMILY. But this girl –

BELLA. This deaf girl is – irrelevant. The last thing you should do – My father – listen to me – my father always says the same thing to me. When I get like (*Gestures to* EMILY.) this. We're all competitive. We're all ambitious. But he says, the thing about envy is, you –

EMILY. What? What about envy? Is this (*Gesticulates to herself, accentuating inverted commas.*) 'Envy'?

BELLA. Yes.

EMILY. Oh.

BELLA. His theory –

EMILY. I thought it was just 'Rage'.

BELLA. Much as I hate to quote him on anything. He says it's fine to suffer envy.

EMILY. But.

BELLA. But – the last thing you should do is, vent your envy. Openly. Because envy is like farts.

EMILY. Envy is like farts?

14

BELLA. Everyone suffers from it. But, if you let it out . . . you don't smell very nice. And everyone moves away from you.

Pause.

EMILY. That's good.

BELLA. I know.

Beat.

Don't dwell on things.

Don't look over your shoulder.

Keep moving on.

Leave what's past behind.

EMILY. Yes. You're right. I know.

I wrote '1995' on a cheque the other day. What was *that* all about?

BELLA*'s phone vibrates. She inspects the caller's number and picks it up.*

BELLA. Hello.

A change in temperature. The other person does all the talking so there are long pauses. As she listens she abstractedly and meticulously moves things upright and into a different order on the table – her lighter, the candle, the packet of cigarettes, the ashtray.

No, I'm just . . .

No, I'm listening.

So he's . . .

Right.

Mnn . . .

What time?

What time was that?

Mmhm . . . mmhm . . .

But that's happened before, hasn't it?

Well, what did Mum say?

OK.

OK.

Well –

Well, if he does –

Well, if he does, then ring me.

Alright.

I'll keep it on.

Bye.

She puts the phone down slowly. EMILY *studies her.* BELLA *looks up.*

I hate the fucking room they've put him in.

Beat.

EMILY. Bella, I'm sorry.

Silence.

Oh Bella . . .

Beat. BELLA *can't speak or she will cry.*

Are you OK?

. . . You're not OK . . .

Listen . . .

Listen to me . . .

There's nothing you can do about it. Nothing.

Pause.

BELLA. I know.

Beat.

Do you think I should be with him now?

Beat.

Do you?

Beat.

EMILY. No. It's your birthday.

BELLA. But should I be with him *now*? Tell me what to do.

EMILY. I can't tell you what to do.

BELLA. Yes you can.

EMILY. I can't.

Beat.

Someone else is with him now, right?

BELLA. One of my brothers. Taking turns. The night shift.

EMILY. And your mum?

BELLA. Oh, of course *she's* there. Always bloody there. The rest of us take turns. Because he's far too sociable to die when someone's in the room. He'll be busy entertaining them.

Beat.

Maybe this is all wrong. Maybe I should go.

EMILY. Then go.

BELLA. Don't agree with me. Don't just *agree* with me. I want you to tell me what to do. You're the doctor. What do you think? You think I should go?

EMILY. Yes.

BELLA. Why?

EMILY. Because I think you should be there. Not here.

BELLA. Why didn't you say so before?

EMILY. Because you didn't ask me before. Bella, I don't know why you're here.

BELLA. Because I organised it.

EMILY. For God's sake, they're your friends. Aren't they? They'll understand.

Beat.

BELLA. I haven't told the others.

Beat.

EMILY. Why not?

BELLA. I just haven't told them.

Beat.

I can't be bothered.

EMILY. You're a fucking idiot sometimes, you know that? You
   should have told them. You need people to know. – Go.
   Now. And it doesn't matter – I'll tell them.

BELLA. I don't want to go. I've been there all day. I can't take
   any more. If he goes, he goes. And don't tell anyone
   anything.

   Beat.

EMILY. You wanted me to tell you what to do. So I'm telling
   you what to do.

BELLA. Listen. I wanted you to talk me *out* of it, not *into* it.

   Her phone rings. She looks at the caller ID.

   People. Ringing.

   The reception's crap in here anyway.

   She mutes the phone. A beat.

EMILY. All you can do is be with him. So go and be with him.

BELLA. I thought there was nothing I could do about it.

EMILY. Bella –

BELLA. We don't get on.

EMILY. He's dying.

BELLA. He's dying and we still don't get on. Nothing's
   changed.

EMILY. You should be there.

BELLA. How do you know I should be there?

EMILY. Because you'll regret it.

BELLA. When was the last time your dad died?

EMILY. Alright, explain it to me. Tell me what it's like.

BELLA. Let's change the subject.

   Music.

EMILY. No, explain it to me, because I don't understand –

BELLA. We're changing the subject –

EMILY. I don't understand so explain it to me!

BELLA. No! He's my dad, not yours!

18

EMILY. Bella!

Music. Loud. FATHER, outside a door. He waits a moment.

FATHER (*shouting*). Did you hear what I said!

He bangs on the door.

Open the door!

Pause.

Open the fucking door!

This is not helping anybody.

The music recedes a little – but thanks to the track, not as a result of being turned down. Pause. Quieter.

Listen to me. You are not qualified to pass judgements on things in this house, things you know nothing about.

This *arrogance* . . .

And this *aggressiveness* . . .

I'm going to say one thing.

One thing.

I pay for everything in this house. I don't see you paying for anything.

I suggest you have a think about that next time you feel a lecture coming on. Lecture your mother if you want but don't think you can lecture me.

If you're not going to come out, then I've got nothing more to say.

Pause. He puts his hand on the door.

It's a pattern with you. A pattern.

Beat. He waits. The door remains shut and –

Lights up on BELLA *and* TOM *together.* EMILY *has left the table.*

BELLA. It is so good to see you again.

Stupid . . .

God, I was stupid.

TOM. So was I.

BELLA (*she means it*). I'm sorry I behaved so badly.

TOM. You didn't behave badly.

BELLA *raises her eyebrows*.

It's OK.

RICHARD *has entered and tiptoes up behind* BELLA, *motioning to* TOM *not to give him away.* BELLA *studies* TOM*'s face*.

BELLA. What?

TOM. Nothing.

BELLA. What? What 'nothing'?

Beat.

What did I say?

RICHARD *puts his hands over her eyes.*

Hey!

Who's this?

Cold hands.

She fingers his sleeves.

I hope this isn't velvet that I'm feeling. Is this velvet?

This is Richard, isn't it. Take your hands off, I don't like being blind.

He bends down to kiss her on the mouth.

RICHARD. Well done. How did you know?

BELLA. Your hands are always so cold.

RICHARD. Cold hands, warm cock.

BELLA. Everyone's cock is warm.

RICHARD. You should know.

He hands her a present.

BELLA (*shakes it*). Feels like something . . . 'little'. This is Tom. Richard. You don't know each other.

TOM. Hi.

They shake.

RICHARD. Hi, hi. Richard. I don't think I know you.

BELLA. That's what I said.

TOM. No. Good to meet you.

RICHARD. Good to meet you. Exactly.

Beat.

I think I'll just . . .

He sits down.

BELLA. Have a drink.

RICHARD *takes a sip of* BELLA*'s glass.*

Not mine.

RICHARD. Jesus! What is this shit?

BELLA. It's very good wine. Tom got it.

RICHARD (*genuinely baffled*). Who's Tom? (*To* TOM.) Oh, Tom of course Tom.

BELLA. Sorry Tom. He's a . . . bit of a . . .

She is struggling with the present.

RICHARD. Let me do it. Women. Hopeless.

BELLA. An arsehole. Used a lot of Sellotape, didn't you? Jesus.

TOM. I'll do it. I've got a penknife –

BELLA. No, no – I can do this fiddly stuff.

They wait for her to open it. A pause while she struggles.

Talk amongst yourselves.

A slight pause.

RICHARD. So, Tom, how do you know Bella?

TOM. Oh, we. We've known each other a while, we –

BELLA (*concentrating on the parcel*). We had an affair.

RICHARD. Really!

Beat.

TOM. Well – we were friends too. Are friends.

RICHARD. Same here, same here. Aren't we all.

Beat.

Right. Now. (*Lifts up bottle.*) Let's finish this crap off and I'll get a different one.

BELLA. Richard.

RICHARD. Sorry. Sorry. He bought it, didn't you. Tom.

TOM. Yes.

RICHARD (*the wine*). It's actually fine.

TOM. No, no, I know nothing about wine.

BELLA. Oh!

It's a wind-chime candle-holder for four candles with little angels that circle round.

Thank you, Richard! How gorgeous . . . Angels . . .

She kisses him.

Do you remember these? I had one when I was little. The heat makes them turn around.

She starts to put it together.

RICHARD. But just out of curiosity. Did the barman recommend it?

TOM. Yes.

RICHARD. I knew it.

TOM. Sorry.

RICHARD. No, no. Not your fault. But – honestly. Don't listen to them.

TOM. Right. Thanks.

BELLA (*engrossed with putting together angel chimes*). Fuck, this is more complicated than it looks.

Her phone rings. She looks at it, picks it up, answers it.

Yeah! Yeah, we're in the bar.

She moves off to take the call. Beat.

RICHARD. So . . . there are other people. (*He starts to assemble the angel chimes.*)

TOM. People.

RICHARD. Coming. It's not just going to be us two.

TOM. Oh no. No, there are other people coming. Girl called Emily's here – she's just gone to the bar.

I just – bumped into Bella.

RICHARD. Right.

TOM. By chance.

RICHARD. I see. Random selection. You'll fit in fine.

TOM. You've . . . known Bella a while?

RICHARD. Yeah.

Beat.

Yeah.

So what do you do, Tom?

TOM. I work in the city. What do you do?

RICHARD. I. Well, it's complicated.

Beat.

I write.

TOM. Really! What do you write? What are you writing at the moment?

RICHARD. Oh, just this thing . . .

Pause.

You know what? Do I have to talk about it? I don't think I want to talk about it. If you talk about things too much you never end up writing them.

TOM. 'Don't tell it – write it.'

RICHARD. That's it!

Beat.

It takes the juice out of it.

TOM. Sure.

RICHARD. And I haven't written that much of it yet. I'm taking it slowly. It's ambitious.

BELLA *is circling, still on her phone. She overhears this.*

BELLA (*to* TOM). You don't want to hear about it anyway, believe me. Fucking boring.

RICHARD (*suspiciously, one eye on* BELLA, *to* TOM). You don't know . . . who else . . . is coming?

BELLA (*to phone*). Richard's writing. Fucking boring.

TOM. Emily – she's already here. Gone to the loo.

BELLA (*to phone*). Yeah. Yeah exactly. My point exactly.

TOM. And someone called Sandy.

RICHARD. Oh Christ. Not Sandy.

TOM. Why what's wrong with Sandy?

RICHARD. Mouthy. Tedious. Opinionated. Thinks she's sexier than she is.

   BELLA *comes back and sits on* RICHARD*'s lap. She talks into her mobile.*

BELLA. Yes, I'm sitting on his lap. No, actually I'm sitting on his face.

   She laughs immoderately.

   I'm not going to tell him that!

   Alright.

   Just get a move on.

   She laughs again. To RICHARD*:*

   Who do you think I'm talking to?

RICHARD. Sandy.

BELLA (*to phone*). No, no one good-looking.

RICHARD. Why's she coming?

BELLA (*to* RICHARD). Because she's my friend. (*She listens to the phone.*) And she's bought us *all* presents.

TOM. Really?

RICHARD (*morosely*). Scratchcards. She's addicted to them. Bella, you could have fucking told me she was coming.

BELLA. And then you wouldn't have come. (*She gets up.*) For God's sake. She hasn't even had anything published yet –

RICHARD. – Neither have I –

BELLA (*to phone*). Have you?

– No, exactly.

(*To* RICHARD.) I don't know why you're so threatened by her.

(*To phone*.) I don't know why he's so threatened by you.

RICHARD. I'm not threatened.

BELLA (*laughs into phone*). Well, yes exactly.

RICHARD. I'm threatened, I'm threatened. Fucking women. Everyone's on their side. (*To* TOM.) Excuse me.

TOM (*with feeling*). No, no. I quite agree.

BELLA (*to phone*). That's right. So you kick 'em in the balls. Yeah.

RICHARD (*decisively*). Let's get pissed.

TOM. Sure.

They down their wine.

RICHARD. So, what were we talking about.

TOM. The fact that you're blocked.

Beat.

RICHARD. I didn't say that. Did I?

Beat.

TOM. Sorry. I don't know anything about writing.

RICHARD. No, you're right. And it's horrible. It's horrible. It means I feel like . . . a fraud. I have no sense of myself.

I'm sorry. It's boring.

TOM. No, it's OK.

Beat.

Listen . . . you just have to wait. The moment'll come. And suddenly it'll be there. You can't force it. You can't force anything. Wait. And it'll happen.

Beat. RICHARD *has put the candles in place in the holder and is about to light them.*

RICHARD. Thanks, Tom. Thanks.

Beat.

What do you do?

TOM. I work in the city.

The candles are lit. BELLA *comes off the phone and comes to sit back down.*

BELLA. Sorry about that.

She stops, seeing the candles and the angels starting to move round slowly. Beat.

Oh . . . How lovely . . .

You know what . . .

. . . I wish I was little again.

They all watch the angels turning.

(*Sitting down, breaking the moment.*) Now, Tom. Sandy. She's just on her way. You don't know her.

TOM. No.

BELLA. So that you know. Don't take anything she says seriously.

TOM. OK.

BELLA. She's a sweet girl.

RICHARD. Bullshit.

BELLA. Deep down. But she feels she has to hide that under this . . . hardness.

RICHARD. She's a sexual kleptomaniac.

TOM. Right.

BELLA. If she's rude to you. I promise you. She doesn't mean it. That's just her way.

RICHARD. She's a pain in the arse.

TOM. OK, no problem.

RICHARD. Led by her twat. No man is safe.

BELLA. Some men find her threatening.

RICHARD. Some men find her a pain in the arse.

BELLA. She asked if you were still blocked, Richard. She said if you are she's got some advice for you.

RICHARD. Did she.

BELLA. She says you should go and have a fag in a McDonald's car park. Because that's where you'll find the working classes. Anywhere you're still allowed to smoke publicly, you'll find good material, she says.

RICHARD. Thanks, thanks, that's very helpful. Very helpful. Does she think I'm incapable of making stuff up? I know she doesn't, because she can't, having no imagination, but I would have thought that's what a *writer* –

BELLA. Also, she asked if this one's set in the future too. Like the others.

Beat.

RICHARD. No, you can tell her it isn't set in the future, this time.

TOM. What?

BELLA (*to* TOM). They're usually set in the future. As a rule.

TOM. Like, *Star Wars* future?

RICHARD. Anything else? Any other tips?

BELLA. No, that was it, I think. Oh no, she wanted to know does anyone die.

RICHARD. Why?

BELLA. She says, don't make anyone die.

RICHARD. And why does she say that.

BELLA. Because it's too easy.

Beat.

TOM. That's true.

BELLA. She's got a point, Richard. Normally your stuff is set in the future, and people tend to die, don't they? Lot of *dying*. As a rule.

RICHARD. Tell her this time, it's not set in the future, and nobody dies in it either.

BELLA. Right. That's probably why you're blocked.

RICHARD. Thanks.

BELLA. I'm only teasing.

RICHARD. Why do you find it funny?

BELLA. Because I can't imagine you being unsuccessful at anything.

RICHARD. Can't you.

She starts to laugh.

BELLA. No really I can't. It just – (*She laughs more.*) – I'm sorry, it just – it tickles me. The thought of you finding something difficult.

I mean, you've already got a great career, why do you have to be 'a writer' too?

She laughs more, and bursts into a coughing fit.

I love the idea of you *struggling* at something.

She laughs and coughs more.

Sorry. God!

She looks at RICHARD.

Oh, come on, Richard, you're a success at just about everything else, why can't I laugh at the one thing you find difficult?

Look! You look so serious about it! OK, I'll stop. I'll stop laughing.

She laughs more.

Sorry, sorry. I've stopped.

Phew, I need water.

She drinks water.

RICHARD. What about you, Bella?

BELLA. What about me?

RICHARD. How's your job? Stimulating? Intellectually demanding? Morally satisfying?

BELLA. Oh screw you.

RICHARD. No really, what are you doing at the moment? Explain it to me. I can never understand what it is that you get paid to do. What is it this week? A new mobile phone? What are you launching?

BELLA. Fuck off.

RICHARD (*to* TOM). Did you know Bella worked for a PR company? Or did she not mention it?

TOM. Really? You know, I've never really understood what PR means. Is it –

RICHARD. My point exactly. What *does* it mean?

BELLA. That's not fair.

RICHARD. Why not?

BELLA. Because I never poked fun at your *job*.

RICHARD. Didn't you?

BELLA. No. I didn't. You're a barrister. I didn't laugh at that.

TOM. A barrister?

BELLA. Yes, did you know Richard worked as a barrister? Or did he not *mention* it? – Now, if you give *that* up, and become a writer full time, then I won't laugh at your 'writing' either. I'll take it seriously. But at the moment, it's OK to laugh at it, because strictly speaking, it's a hobby.

RICHARD. Really. I thought that's what your job was.

Pause.

BELLA. That wasn't kind.

RICHARD. It wasn't meant to be.

Beat.

BELLA (*suddenly inflamed*). Fuck you.

RICHARD. Ah lighten up. Christ, it's OK for you to piss yourself over my writing, and I'm supposed to take it like a man, but if I joke about your job – if it *is* a job – sorry, sorry, joking –

BELLA. But it isn't a joke. That's what you think. It's the same joke every time. You wouldn't make the joke if it wasn't what you thought.

RICHARD. You know, Bella, your trouble is you rise so easily.

It's irresistible. That's why I *do* it every time. Guaranteed results.

BELLA. But you weren't joking.

RICHARD. I was.

BELLA. You meant it. It's what you think.

RICHARD. It's a *joke*.

BELLA. It's what you think, Richard, you're not fucking joking, fucking admit it!

Beat.

RICHARD. OK, it's a waste-of-time mindless job. I can't understand why you're doing it. Satisfied?

Beat.

TOM. I've heard it's well paid, is that –

RICHARD (*to* BELLA). You wanted to know, I'll tell you. I can't understand why an intelligent girl like you is doing a job like that. (*To* TOM.) She's wasting her mind, she's wasting her intelligence, she's wasting her abilities.

BELLA. You know, when you talk like that, you're not actually praising me, you're putting me down?

RICHARD. I'm putting you *down*?

BELLA. You're putting me down and patronising me.

RICHARD. How am I putting you down? I'm giving you a compliment. I'm saying I think you're too good for your job –

BELLA. What makes you think *you* can tell *me* I'm too good for my job?

RICHARD. Because I think you could do better.

BELLA. Why do you think you can say that to me? Because you think *you're* better than me. That's why. It isn't a compliment, it's a put-down.

RICHARD. I'm trying to say you're talented and you're in the wrong job and you think that's a put-down.

BELLA. Because deep down, it is!

RICHARD (*to* TOM). What do I have to do to get her to take a fucking compliment?

TOM (*taken aback*). Jesus, you two . . .

EMILY comes back to the table with wine.

EMILY (*smiles*). Hi. (*She extends her hand to* RICHARD.) I'm Emily.

RICHARD *stands up*.

RICHARD. Wow.

He shakes her hand.

EMILY. What?

RICHARD. Great teeth.

EMILY. Thanks.

She puts down a wine bottle.

More wine!

She sits down.

RICHARD (*to* BELLA). See? It's not that difficult. She can do it.

EMILY. What?

RICHARD. Take a compliment. Sorry, hi, I'm Richard.

EMILY. Hi. Oh, 'Richard'. Hi. Pleased to meet you.

TOM (*aside, to* BELLA). Are you OK?

BELLA (*aside*). Yeah yeah, this is always happening.

Beat.

EMILY. What have I missed?

BELLA. Nothing. He's a cunt.

RICHARD is staring at EMILY.

RICHARD. Wait a minute.

I know you. I *know* you. We've met before.

Beat.

EMILY. I . . . don't think we have.

RICHARD. No, we have. We have definitely met.

EMILY. Have we?

RICHARD. Where was it?

I've got a feeling it was at a party, or something . . .

Was it at a party?

EMILY. I don't think it was at a party.

RICHARD. Maybe . . . at a dinner party? A long time ago. Or is it just that you *remind* me of someone –

BELLA. Oh shut up.

EMILY. What?

BELLA. He does this to every pretty girl, ignore it. (*To* RICHARD.) She may look like a bimbo, but she's not. Try something else.

RICHARD (*ignoring* BELLA). My God, I've got it. I know who you are.

EMILY. Who am I?

RICHARD. You don't remember?

Beat.

EMILY. No.

BELLA. That's right, don't give him any help.

Beat.

RICHARD. You're a doctor.

EMILY. Yes.

RICHARD. At Chelsea and Westminster.

EMILY. That's right.

Pause.

Oh my God.

BELLA. What?

RICHARD. Do you remember now?

EMILY. . . . Richard.

RICHARD. . . . Emily . . . This is . . .

They embrace.

I can't believe it.

EMILY. You're OK now?

RICHARD. I'm OK.

TOM. You know each other?

EMILY. I treated Richard. When I was training.

RICHARD. She was marvellous.

EMILY. Oh please . . . I made a complete tit of myself.

They laugh.

BELLA. Ha ha. Very funny.

RICHARD. What? You think we're winding you up? We're not.

BELLA. Right.

RICHARD. I swear we're not. Emily treated me about a year ago. I went into A&E with something.

BELLA. What?

RICHARD. What?

BELLA. What did you go into A&E with?

RICHARD. I'm not telling you.

Beat.

BELLA. Why won't you tell me?

EMILY. It's true, I did see him.

BELLA. OK. So tell me what was wrong with him then.

Beat.

EMILY. I can't tell you that.

BELLA. Why not?

EMILY. I'm under the Hippocratic Oath.

BELLA. Don't be ridiculous.

EMILY. I'm not. It's true. I can't.

BELLA. Bollocks.

RICHARD. I was panicking about something.

BELLA. What? Writer's block?

Beat.

Panicking about what?

RICHARD. That's between me and Emily.

Beat.

So you believe us now?

Beat.

EMILY. I never thought I'd see you again.

They laugh.

RICHARD. Emily had a certain . . . *je ne sais quoi.*

EMILY (*to* RICHARD *in a French accent*). Non, non. I just treated you like any other patient.

They laugh.

RICHARD (*in a French accent*). No, really, I mean it. A *je ne sais quoi.* (*Normal.*) Seriously, I can't believe I've met you again. Bella, I had no idea you knew her. How come you've never introduced us before?

Small beat.

BELLA. Because I thought you'd get off with each other.

RICHARD. Why did you think that?

BELLA. I don't know. Why *did* I think that?

Beat.

RICHARD. You're annoyed that Emily treated me. You're annoyed that we've met each other. Why? Why does that annoy you?

Beat.

BELLA. Because you won't tell me what was wrong with you.

RICHARD. Why should I?

Beat.

You don't tell me everything. And I don't have to tell you everything.

BELLA. I do.

RICHARD. No you don't. Now you know what it feels like.

SANDY *comes in*.

SANDY. Hello, hello, here I am! Sorry I'm late! Hello! And presents . . . for everyone.

Sees TOM.

Wow, who's he?

TOM. Hello. Tom.

SANDY. Tom. Hello.

Hello. I don't know you.

EMILY. Hi. Emily.

SANDY. But I know you. (RICHARD.)

RICHARD. Hello.

SANDY. Hello.

She distributes scratchcards.

Here you are . . . here you are . . . scratchcards . . . Bought too many . . . Thought there'd be more of us . . . But I see it's a 'select few'. Hope you all like these. We've all got to do them at the same time. Like fireworks. Or maybe we should spread them out over the night. Like fireworks. What do you think? Bella – (*Kissing her*.) happy birthday! Champagne? What're we going to have? What's the tradition, on Bella's birthday?

RICHARD. An argument.

SANDY. Oh I see! Are we having it yet? (*To* BELLA.) I couldn't think what to buy you so I got you twenty-nine, plus a lucky dip. And some fags. You're bound to win something.

BELLA. Thanks so much.

SANDY. That's why I'm so late. Shopping.

BELLA. You smell like you've been in the pub.

SANDY. What are you, my dad?

BELLA. How many pints have you had?

SANDY. *Pints?* None at all. I've been shopping. Oxford Street is so *violent*. I've had a nightmare. You know how I got here? Well, in an act of false bravado, I –

RICHARD. Isn't bravado always false?

Beat.

SANDY. Look at him. He's clever. He's a *writer*.

Anyway. In an act of false bravado, I tried to cycle here.

BELLA. In those shoes?

SANDY. What is *wrong* with you two tonight?

BELLA. You're a compulsive liar.

SANDY. Fucking *questioning* everything. Why don't you let me finish my bloody story? Firstly, I always cycle in these shoes. The shoes weren't the problem. It was the fucking pedestrians. Getting in my way. I had to get off, wheel it. And then it was raining. And then this tramp stopped me, when I tried to get past her she grabbed hold of my bicycle basket and wouldn't let go, I was standing there holding the bike, she was standing there holding the bike, she wasn't going to let go until I gave her the money.

TOM. What did you do?

SANDY. I just said to her, I said, (*Straight into* TOM*'s face.*) 'Get your fucking hands off my bicycle basket *this instant* or I'll punch you right between the eyes.'

TOM. Wow.

EMILY. And what happened?

SANDY. She took 'em off. *Immediately.* I just hate all this aggression, you know?

TOM. Yeah.

SANDY. All these aggressive people.

RICHARD *gets up.*

(*Cooing.*) Oh *Richard*!

RICHARD. What?

SANDY. Sit down. I've only just *got* here. Where are you going?

RICHARD. Getting some cigarettes. Need them, now that you're here.

SANDY. What about getting me a *drink*? – Sulking about something, isn't he. I can see it in his face. What's wrong, Richard? Had a bad day at court?

EMILY. Court?

SANDY. Did you lose your case? Or are you just *fed up* with the outfit?

RICHARD. Oh Jesus.

SANDY. It suits you! Has he shown you?

BELLA. Sandy, drop it.

SANDY. Where's his bag?

She roots around under the table.

I just love this.

She unzips his bag and hunts through it.

RICHARD. Sandy –

SANDY. Where is it? You did come straight from court, didn't you? (*Producing a lawyer's wig.*) Put it on, Richard. (*To the others.*) He looks *so* funny in it.

RICHARD. Sandy.

SANDY. Go on, Richard. Please.

RICHARD. It is actually against the law.

SANDY. Come on, Richard.

BELLA. Sandy –

SANDY (*by now on* RICHARD*'s side of the table and able to put the wig rakishly on his head*). Isn't it hilarious? What is it, Richard? You should be PROUD, you're a lawyer, you earn SO much money –

RICHARD *stands with the wig on his head, dignified. The others suppress laughter.*

RICHARD. I'm glad you find my job so amusing.

EMILY. So you're a lawyer as well?

SANDY. Yes! What do you think this is? Fancy dress?

Although, Richard, you could also get *very* lucrative work as a kissogram.

They laugh.

RICHARD. Have you quite finished? Laughing at my job?

BELLA. Honestly, Richard. I'm sure you're impressive. In court. It does have a certain . . . *je ne sais quoi.*

They all laugh.

RICHARD. I thought you wanted to be a lawyer, Bella.

Beat.

BELLA. Yes. Once upon a time.

RICHARD. So I don't know why you're laughing.

BELLA. Because I didn't make it. Thanks for reminding me.

RICHARD. I wouldn't worry. You're probably earning much more than me now.

Beat.

BELLA. Oh I see, back to my fucking job again. Your point?

RICHARD. I'm talking about what you earn. What are you earning?

BELLA. I'm earning a lot.

RICHARD. And that's all that matters.

BELLA. It's something.

Beat.

What do you want me to say? I hate my job. I wish I was a lawyer.

I envy you. Well done.

BELLA *gets up from the table, lights a cigarette. Pause.*

SANDY. Nice one, Richard.

RICHARD. If that's the way you feel about it, why the fuck did you give it up?

The others shift uncomfortably.

BELLA (*turning on him*). Christ, *this* again? I told you, because I wasn't good enough, because I would have failed the exams, because I wasn't good enough.

RICHARD. Crap.

BELLA. We've *had* this argument. We've *had* it.

Beat.

Because I knew I wasn't going to be good enough. So I got out. Sooner rather than later.

RICHARD (*gets up*). You didn't 'know' anything. How could you? You didn't wait to find out.

Suddenly, FATHER *is standing there. Elated. A glass of wine in his hand. The atmosphere is jovial, drunken.*

FATHER. She doesn't want to listen to me –

BELLA. Oh *God* . . .

FATHER. I mean it! You, will, be *great* . . .

BELLA. You're *pissed*, Dad!

Stop it –

FATHER. I'm sixty . . .

BELLA. Self-pity starting, wait for it –

FATHER. And I mean this . . . I could die tomorrow –

BELLA. Five four three two one –

FATHER. – it would be perfectly alright by me –

BELLA (*singing*). 'Ding dong, the witch is dead, the witch is dead the witch is dead – '

FATHER. Fuck off, I've had enough of this, it's my turn! (*He holds up four fingers.*) This means four words.

BELLA. I know what it bloody well means.

FATHER. Good. And it's a . . .

He mimes singing into a mike.

BELLA. Blow job. (FATHER *shoots her a filthy look.*)

FATHER. A song, moron. A pop song.

He makes a circle in the air with his arms. RICHARD *has joined* BELLA, *has his arms around her waist.*

RICHARD. The world. Teach the world to sing in perfect harmony.

FATHER *shakes head.*

Oh. No. Um.

FATHER *makes gesture again.*

World. Um. Universe. Galaxy. Circle. Hands.

FATHER *keeps shaking head in frustration and repeating gesture.*

What? What? I can't think of anything else. Circle. No, I've already said that.

FATHER. Give him some help! Some help! Why is he the only one trying?

BELLA. Hoop.

FATHER *shakes head in frustration.*

Swimming. (*Sings R.E.M. song.*) 'Night Swimming. Deseeerves a quiet night.'

FATHER. No, for Christ's sake. Have I said 'first word, second word'? No! This means I'm going to do . . . (*He makes the gesture again, vehemently.*)

BELLA (*becoming intrigued*). Ballet?

FATHER. Are you fucking deaf? I said –

BELLA. Dad. Dad. Dad. Surely the whole point of charades is that you're not meant to *say* anything.

Beat.

FATHER. I know, but you're both being so bloody *slow.*

He makes the gesture again. They gaze at him in bafflement. He glares at them, then –

This (*The gesture.*) means that I'm going to do the whole thing. Got it? I can see I'm playing with total amateurs. Wonderful. Here we go. The whole thing. Coming up.

He erases the sourness, with some effort, from his face, and begins to mime laughing. As he does this he starts to walk backwards out of the room, until he has exited. They wait.

BELLA. He *loves* you.

RICHARD. Is he coming back? What the fuck was *that*?

BELLA. God. Um. I've no idea. Any ideas?

40

RICHARD. Yeah. Let's hide. Quick, before he comes back.

They laugh, look at each other. Beat.

BELLA (*singing softly*). 'Walking back to happiness' . . . *That's* what he was doing.

They look at each other. Lights fade. Back to the restaurant. An abrupt change in mood. BELLA *has gone from inflamed to depressed, sitting with her head in her hands.* SANDY *turns on her.*

SANDY. *Why* are you letting him bully you?

BELLA. I was bullying him.

SANDY. No you weren't. Why are you letting *him* bully *you*?

BELLA. Because he had a point.

SANDY. No he did not.

BELLA. He's right.

SANDY. No he's not. What's he right about?

BELLA. He's right about why I dropped out of the law course.

SANDY. He's not right. He's not right. What do you mean, 'he's right'? Don't listen to Richard. Listen to me.

BELLA. Richard knows the way my head works.

SANDY. No he doesn't. No he *doesn't*. I can't bear this, Bella. You're not allowed to be brainwashed by him any more, you're not allowed to be bullied by him any more, you're not fucking him any more. You've got a mind of your own. He doesn't know the way your head works. *You* know the way your head works.

BELLA. Yes. And so does he.

SANDY. Stop it! You don't belong to him any more! I mean, this is what this is all about! You do realise that, don't you? This is all about sex.

BELLA. It's because I made fun of his writing.

SANDY. And that gives him the right to slag your job and tell you you're self-destructive?

BELLA. I am self-destructive.

SANDY. So you dropped out of a law course. Years ago. Big

deal. You've got a perfectly good job in PR instead. Earning a fuck of a lot more than anyone else around this table.

BELLA. He's right. It's a stupid mindless waste-of-time job.

SANDY. Listen to me, will you? This isn't about your job. This is about sex.

BELLA. This has nothing to do with sex.

SANDY. This has *everything* to do with sex. This is about men and women. It's because he's a man and you're a woman.

BELLA. Well, then how do you explain the fact that my *dad* said exactly the same thing?

SANDY. Because your dad's a man too. Isn't he?

BELLA. That's not what this is about!

SANDY. It is! Men like telling women what to do. The sexual ego is a very fragile thing. Richard's fucked you. He's not fucking you any more. So he feels two things. The two things all men feel about their exes. Vulnerable. And proprietorial.

EMILY. Women feel that too, don't they?

SANDY (*coldly*). Hold on, let me finish. They're like dogs. Richard has to pretend he still owns you. Which he does by bullying you. Spraying.

TOM. Dogs don't spray. That's cats.

SANDY. Dogs do spray. They spray urine. Same thing. Why? To tell people like – like you, say (TOM.) – to keep off. Typical male.

TOM. Who? Me or him?

BELLA. Can we stop it now?

SANDY. What?

BELLA. Reading the entrails. It's dead. Over.

SANDY. Tell Richard that, not me. You know what it is? It was a *boyfriend* who offered you the job in PR when you gave up the law. Whatsisname.

That's what really gets him. Another man. Also, how long were you with Richard? It takes the same number of years to get *over* a relationship as the years you were *in* it. I'm right. You know I am. And I predict, the next thing he'll do, he'll try to woo you. (*To* EMILY.) You're just his type.

EMILY. What do you mean?

SANDY. He'll sit next to you and he'll tell you all about his ex-wife. I bet you. I bet you a scratchcard. He's always going on about having been married. I think he thinks it makes him sexy. You feel like saying, look, mate, we've all had our marriages. You're nothing special.

TOM. Oh, have you been married too?

SANDY. Not yet, but you know what I mean.

Beat.

Still, at least he's got rid of that terrible ponytail. I mean, what on earth made him think a ponytail was a good idea? Did he think it made him look more like a '*writer*'?

Beat.

Well, I think it is true to say – you lift up a ponytail, underneath it, you *will* find an arsehole.

BELLA. Can we *stop* fucking talking about him?

SANDY. And whatever he says, he *hates* the fact that you earn more than him.

RICHARD *approaches*.

BELLA. Sandy –

SANDY (*in response to the unspoken plea*). Alright, alright, I'm not going to get involved, I *won't* start lecturing him –

BELLA. No, you just save the lectures for me.

SANDY. That's what friends are for.

RICHARD. Tequila!

He is carrying a tray of shots. The others respond appropriately as the shots are taken and drunk. RICHARD *sits down – next to* EMILY.

SANDY (*brightly*). So! Richard! Are you getting laid?

RICHARD. Maybe I am, maybe I'm not. Maybe I don't want to talk about it.

SANDY. Maybe you're not.

RICHARD. Maybe I'm not. (*Passing the question on.*)

Emily?

EMILY. What?

SANDY *clears her throat, gives* BELLA *a meaningful look.*

RICHARD. Are you seeing anybody?

EMILY. Me? No, I'm not.

SANDY. Bella? Are you –

BELLA. No.

RICHARD. And Sandy? I suppose you're getting laid.

SANDY. Actually, I am.

Beat.

Well, we seem to have been pretty much round the table.
Tom? Are you getting laid?

TOM. No, as a matter of fact, I'm not.

SANDY. Right.

Beat. In an undertone:

Doesn't say much, does he?

Beat.

Are we going to order some food or what? Bella, jack over
the menus. I see you lost the ponytail, Richard.

RICHARD. Yes. It made me look like an arsehole. So tell us
about your boyfriend.

SANDY. Well, I don't like that expression.

RICHARD (*chants*). 'Sandy's got a boyfriend, Sandy's got a
boyfriend – (*In an undertone.*) The poor bastard . . . '

SANDY (*cuts in*). Actually, he's a singer. A countertenor.

BELLA. Good in bed?

SANDY. Quite. (*Thinks about this.*) I mean, I'm better.

RICHARD. God, don't tell me, I can imagine it, the
marathons, sitting on his face, all night long, him trying
desperately to *survive* –

BELLA (*cuts in*). What does he look like?

RICHARD. – with a *snorkel* –

BELLA. What does he look like when he sings?

RICHARD (*sings, in countertenor pitch, atonally*). 'Little Miss Muffet, sat on a tuffet . . . '

SANDY (*cuts in*). Don't know. Haven't seen him sing yet. Anyway, that's enough about him. Tell us about the silent beauty. Bella. Who is he? Where have you been hiding him?

Beat.

TOM. Sorry, me?

RICHARD (*putting his arm around* TOM). Yes, Tom, Bella. Who is Tom?

Beat.

BELLA. An old flame. He's an old flame.

Beat.

SANDY. Really! An old flame. I *see*.

TOM. We –

BELLA. What do you mean, you *'see'*?

SANDY. That explains a lot.

BELLA. Explains a lot?

SANDY. Why didn't you tell me before? (*To* RICHARD.) Did you know that?

RICHARD. Yes, I did. As of tonight.

SANDY. I *see*. Explains the way *you've* (RICHARD.) been behaving, for a start.

RICHARD. I beg your pardon?

SANDY. I must say, I'm surprised. I mean, normally I sense these things.

I didn't see *that* one coming.

BELLA. Really.

SANDY. Not from a mile off.

BELLA. And why not.

SANDY. Well . . . How can I put this . . . He's not exactly your *type*, is he?

I mean, I don't like your type. Because come on, Bella. Usually you don't have much taste. Take Richard. Now he's nothing like Richard, is he? No . . . (*Looking at him.*) . . . There's definitely something about him.

Beat.

TOM. What's going on?

Beat.

RICHARD. Why are you talking about him in the third person?

SANDY. Why are you?

Beat.

BELLA. What do you mean, 'there's something about him'?

SANDY. Well. He's more my type, really.

BELLA. What do you mean, more your type?

Beat. TOM *clears his throat, shifts uneasily in his seat.*

TOM. OK, shall we –

SANDY. That's the type that *I* normally go for.

BELLA. Look – Sandy – just leave it, will you?

Beat.

SANDY. *Leave* it?

BELLA. Yeah. He's an ex. My ex. So just leave it.

Beat.

SANDY. Jesus, Bella, what's wrong with you tonight?

Beat.

I was only talking –

BELLA. Yes, you were only talking. That's the fucking problem. Only talking.

It's all you talk about. It's all you think about.

Sex, sex, sex. I'm fed up with it. Fed up!

Everyone trying to fuck each other!

You're as bad as each other.

You trying to fuck him. Him trying to fuck her.

Fuck, fuck, fuck.

No one knows what to say.

Why am I here?

Beat. Lights up on FATHER.

I mean it, why am I here?

Why are *you* here?

Beat.

SANDY. Because we love you.

We love you.

Lights up on FATHER. *Sitting. In the dressing gown of the first scene. He turns to* BELLA.

FATHER. Because you wanted to talk about / it.

BELLA (*dully*). / No. I don't want to talk about it.

Pause.

I don't want to think about it. I don't understand why you're doing this. You're the one – *you're* the one – who wants to talk about it.

Beat.

I thought it was a stroke.

FATHER. I know.

Beat.

Look, I'm not going to try surgery because it wouldn't make any difference.

BELLA. It would make a difference to *me*.

FATHER. I don't understand why you think it *matters* so much.

BELLA. Because it matters. It matters.

FATHER. It doesn't. That's where you're wrong.

Beat.

Nice to see you, anyway.

I see you've taken up smoking again.

BELLA. Big deal.

FATHER. Yeah. Big deal. You think that doesn't matter.

Beat.

Look, it's not as if I'm *enjoying* this. It's not exactly *fun*.

BELLA. For Christ's sake, Dad.

FATHER. I can't see anything on either side. (*Holds up his hands on either side.*) All I can see is this. (*Waves hand to indicate straight beam in front of his face.*)

BELLA. It's called tunnel vision.

FATHER. Hilarious.

Beat.

And haloes. Everyone seems to have a halo. So fucking distracting.

Beat.

There's *too much* time.

BELLA. What do you want me to say?

FATHER. I don't expect you to get angry. This isn't something to get angry about.

BELLA. Oh yes it is. It is. Jesus, Jesus, Jesus. I mean, this is what I can't stand.

FATHER. What?

BELLA. This *self-pity*. This fucking self-pity. 'It's no *fun*.'

There's something you can do. Why don't you do it?

FATHER. Because it's *not going to work*. Christ, Bella! They'd have to mutilate the brain to get at it.

All surgery can get me is three more months. And I don't want them. Why can't you get that into your thick skull?

Why do you have to turn everything into an ultimatum?

BELLA. Well, I hate to point it out, but that's what we're dealing with here, isn't it, Dad. An ultimatum. There *is* an ultimatum. I hate to point it out but to be honest –

FATHER. No! Don't! You've done that since you were thirteen. I can't stand it. 'To be honest.' You only *ever* say that when you want to disagree with someone.

Beat.

It's in here. It's in here and now you're in here too. Both of you. Trying to get your own way.

Why can't you leave it be?

BELLA. Because I'm not going to *lie* to you. Everyone else is. I'm not going to. Because it's not too late to change your mind. They can try and cut it out.

I want you to try it.

I know there's some sentimental idea about your wishes. But what about *our* wishes?

Beat.

You're being selfish.

FATHER. And you're being Bella.

They stare at each other.

The restaurant table. SANDY *is just sitting back down.*

SANDY. She's gone to the loos. She won't talk to me.

RICHARD. It's not your fault.

SANDY. Fuck, I mean, I don't think it's my fault.

EMILY. No, it's both your faults.

SANDY. What do you know about it?

EMILY. I know she's having a hard time at the moment.

Beat.

SANDY. I don't think I said anything wrong.

EMILY. She's got a lot on her mind.

RICHARD. You didn't say anything wrong. Listen, she acted like I was trying to wind her up too.

TOM. You were. Both of you were.

RICHARD. Well, what's wrong with that?

SANDY. Why's she being so touchy?

EMILY. She probably felt 'vulnerable' and 'proprietorial'.

SANDY. I was only trying to get her to be more honest with herself.

RICHARD. I thought that's what I was doing.

SANDY. Well, so was I. She obviously still likes you, (TOM.) why can't she admit it?

EMILY. It's not about that.

SANDY. Of course it's about that. I know Bella. I mean, I *know* her.

RICHARD. So do I.

EMILY. We *all* fucking know Bella.

SANDY. Not like *I* know her.

TOM. Listen, I don't care, OK? If you discuss me. I don't give a fuck. But it upset her.

RICHARD. Aah, don't worry about Bella's feelings. Tough as old boots. Anyway, does she ever worry about anyone else's feelings?

SANDY. No.

RICHARD. No. Exactly. I mean, Christ, she's been in there for twenty-five minutes.

EMILY. I think she might be crying.

Pause.

SANDY. Why?

Beat.

EMILY. Because she's upset.

RICHARD. . . . I mean, 'feelings' . . . we've all got fucking *feelings*, who gives a fuck? Grow up.

SANDY. Yeah, I mean, what about my feelings? She's made me feel like shit. What does she think, I'm going to make a pass at him? That's not what I was doing.

RICHARD. Wasn't it?

TOM. Sorry, who is 'him'? Me?

Beat.

SANDY. Maybe I should go and get her.

RICHARD. Don't bother. Let her stew. That's the best thing to do with Bella. She'll cool off. Christ, I should know. Why do you think none of us have ever met any of each other before?

EMILY. Why?

RICHARD. Because she's a control freak.

EMILY. Control freak?

SANDY. *We've* met each other.

RICHARD. We don't count. (*Explanatory*.) I'm never going to try to get off with you.

SANDY. Thanks.

RICHARD. You know what I mean. She doesn't want *me* to flirt with *her*. (EMILY.) She doesn't want *you* (SANDY.) to flirt with *him*. (TOM.) She wants to control everything.

TOM. Why?

RICHARD. She's scared of not getting all the love.

Beat.

TOM (*to* RICHARD). You must've known Bella a long time?

RICHARD. Oh God yes.

TOM. You went out with each other?

RICHARD. Sort of depends what you mean by that. Five years. On, off, hot, cold, yes, no. Backwards and forwards. After I broke up with my wife. I got married young.

SANDY (*covertly passing* EMILY *a scratchcard*). There you go.

TOM. Right.

A pause. SANDY *bites into a Kettle-Chip-style crisp loudly*. RICHARD *looks at her irritably*.

RICHARD. It didn't work. Bella and me.

EMILY. Yeah.

Beat.

RICHARD (*suspiciously*). Yeah what?

EMILY. Yeah I know.

RICHARD. What do you know?

EMILY. That she fucked things up. She fucked it up.

RICHARD. That's right. She did fuck it up.

SANDY. Really?

RICHARD. Yeah. Damn right she fucked it up. She fucked someone else. *That's* how much she fucked it up.

Beat.

Still, I'm over it now.

It's all good material.

SANDY (*abstractedly scratching a scratchcard*). Best way to look at it.

Beat.

i.e. you were the one who got hurt . . .

. . . Hooray!

She is looking at the scratchcard.

Ten quid. I'll give it to Bella.

RICHARD (*to* TOM). So what about you?

TOM. Me?

RICHARD. You and Bella.

SANDY. Yeah. Now that Bella's not here, you can tell us. What happened there?

Beat.

RICHARD. Are we gossiping?

SANDY. Yes, I think we are.

RICHARD. OK.

EMILY. Can't you two *leave* it?

SANDY. What are you, his wife?

EMILY *is silenced. They wait expectantly.*

RICHARD (*a prompt*). Who got hurt?

SANDY. In other words.

RICHARD. Yes, give us the broad sketch.

52

TOM. Broad sketch?

SANDY. Venn diagram.

Beat.

TOM. Look, I don't think –

EMILY. He doesn't want to say. (*To* TOM.) You don't have to say.

RICHARD. Get on with it.

Beat.

TOM. There is no story. It's not interesting.

RICHARD. It is.

SANDY. It *is*.

RICHARD. See? I'm interested. She's interested.

SANDY. We're all interested.

RICHARD. But we won't use it.

TOM. *Use* it?

SANDY. No, we won't. As material. Don't worry. He can't. (RICHARD.) I won't.

TOM. I said. There's no story.

Beat.

There's no story.

SANDY. What, you were never really boyfriend and girlfriend.

RICHARD. Bella was already with somebody.

SANDY. You were Bella's bit on the side.

RICHARD. You were Bella's / toy boy.

TOM. / No.

Beat.

No. It was the other way round. I already had a girlfriend. And – then I met Bella.

SANDY. Oh right. So you left your girlfriend. For Bella.

TOM. I didn't leave my girlfriend. I left Bella.

I left Bella. And stayed with my girlfriend. Instead of Bella.

Beat.

And then that ended as well.

RICHARD. Oh I see.

TOM. They both got upset. When they found out about each other.

EMILY. Oh dear.

SANDY. Oh dear.

Beat.

Mind you, I've done things like that.

TOM. Like what? Been unfaithful?

SANDY. Well, yeah.

Haven't we all?

Beat.

RICHARD. Why did you leave Bella?

TOM. I knew it wasn't right. It was all wrong.

Pause.

I could tell she didn't take it seriously. I could tell that something was wrong. Because of . . .

The way she looked at me. Sometimes.

Beat.

The way she looked. When I kissed her. Sometimes.

Beat. The menu:

Maybe we should –

RICHARD. But anyway you preferred your girlfriend.

TOM. No. I preferred Bella.

RICHARD. But you stayed –

TOM. With my girlfriend.

Beat.

RICHARD. Why did it end with your girlfriend?

TOM. Because I couldn't forget about Bella.

Beat.

SANDY. Tom . . . I think you made the wrong decision.

TOM. Shall we talk about something else?

They stare before them in silence, at the circling angels. Silence.

RICHARD. Are they going clockwise or anticlockwise?

Beat.

EMILY. Clockwise. No, anticlockwise.

SANDY. Yeah.

RICHARD. Clockwise.

Beat.

Look. You can . . . anticlockwise.

Beat.

If you stare at them and concentrate.

He shifts the angels a little distance from them. To a higher spot – on a ledge or alcove.

You can make them go round both ways. Backwards and forwards.

They stare at the angels. Pause.

BELLA *and her* FATHER.

FATHER. I still love you.

BELLA. Yes. You love me because I'm part of you.

The restaurant.

SANDY. You trick your eyes.

EMILY. Clockwise.

RICHARD. See it both ways round.

SANDY. Yeah.

RICHARD. Anticlockwise.

Beat.

SANDY. I'm feeling bad, I'm feeling bad about Bella. I think I get it. I mean, I think I get what's wrong.

Beat.

I think she's still in love with you.

TOM. Me? Or him?

SANDY. You . . . I'd better go and apologise to her. I didn't
realise.

Beat. To TOM:

I'm sorry.

I'll just . . .

She downs a glass of wine.

God. Apologising. I hate it.

She pours another glass of wine. To EMILY:

Do you think I should go?

EMILY. Yes.

SANDY. Right . . .

She sips her glass of wine. Beat.

EMILY (*decisively*). I'll come with you. Come on.

They get up and go. A pause.

RICHARD. Tom – one last question – when did this thing –
you and Bella?

TOM. Oh . . . about . . . nearly two years ago.

RICHARD. Duration?

TOM. End of the summer until Christmas time? I'm guessing.

RICHARD. Right. I see.

Beat.

You were Bella's bit on the side while she was with me.
Thanks. Thanks.

Beat.

That explains a lot.

They stare at the angels, circling in front of them.

BELLA*'s* FATHER *is holding a book. He speaks slowly,
haltingly, with difficulty.*

FATHER. 'And then . . . with difficulty . . . going . . . were
beaten . . . by means of . . . underneath . . . the . . . ditches
. . . with . . . difficulty.'

This doesn't make sense.

And your *handwriting* . . . Look at this.

What was the Latin?

No, look back at the Latin.

Mulieres.

It's plural.

And who are 'they'?

No, not soldiers.

No, not captains.

Not vases. You're being silly now.

I'll give you a clue. They're female. Female.

'Trouble and strife.'

Beat.

I'm bored now. Wives. The wives.

You rush too much. When you rush it you make stupid mistakes.

You need to use your head.

Think harder, rush less.

He shuts the book and holds it shut.

End of Act One.

ACT TWO

Snap up on the restaurant. Everyone talking at once. It is later.
BELLA *is back at the table. Scratched scratchcards on the*
floor. The food has arrived. They are all drunker.

All simultaneously over each other:

RICHARD. / No OK, OK, I know what it is, I know what it is.
I know what it is! Why isn't anyone listening to me?

SANDY. / Bullshit, bullshit, bullshit . . .

BELLA. / Don't tell me – don't tell me. I know what I think. I
know what I think. I know. You –

EMILY. / I don't think that's fair. I don't think I –

TOM. / Wait, wait wait a minute. This is – this is –

RICHARD (*bellows*). SHUT UP AND LISTEN!

They are silenced.

Look at it from our point of view! The real problem is –
you treat us like sex objects.

SANDY. In your dreams.

RICHARD. No, I'm absolutely serious. You – women . . . treat
us like sex objects. And *that's* what the problem is.

EMILY. Women do not treat men like sex objects.

RICHARD. Listen, Emily.

EMILY. Yes, Richard.

RICHARD. What do people do when they're treating someone
like a sex object? They reduce them to their physical, sexual
characteristics and nothing more. Now who does that? I'll
tell you who – women do that. Men – don't.

Resistance here from SANDY *and* BELLA, *which he raises*
his voice to talk over.

It is a total fallacy that men discuss their conquests. Listen.
We are actually extremely discreet.

58

BELLA. Bullshit. Absolute bullshit.

RICHARD. No, listen.

BELLA. 'Listen' 'Listen' 'Listen' – We're not fucking deaf, you know.

RICHARD. Listen. No, I mean it. OK, here's an example.

SANDY. When you're talking to a deaf person do you know what the sign language for bullshit is?

She makes it at BELLA.

RICHARD. Here's an example –

BELLA. Or cunt? (*She makes it.*)

RICHARD (*continues, ignoring them*). – You go off for half an hour – and by the way, I'm *not* talking about the mega-sulk in the loo just now although I *could* –

BELLA. I've got a lot on my mind.

RICHARD. Yeah, yeah. I mean, you're a shit host at the best of times but this was something else. What were you *doing* in there?

SANDY. Oh shut up, Richard.

BELLA. None of your business.

EMILY. Well, she's back now, so let's just celebrate that, shall we – (*She drinks.*)

RICHARD (*interrupting*). *Before* you even started stropping out – that *brief* period at the beginning of this evening – you left Tom and *me* on our own for ten fucking minutes while you chat to Sandy on the phone. Now. My point is. Tom and I. We've only just met each other. We only have one thing in common.

Beat.

We both know what you're like in bed. But do we discuss that? The one obvious icebreaker? No! We struggle on without.

BELLA. Oh for –

RICHARD (*talking over her*). Now, would you and Sandy do that? No! You'd be talking length, breadth, hair growth pattern.

BELLA. Absolute rubbish.

RICHARD. I'm sorry, Bella . . .

EMILY (*with finality*). He's right.

RICHARD. . . . There's too much evidence against you. I've never forgotten you describing – God, it wasn't even his cock – Jack's . . . (*With distaste.*) bumhole to me. In intimate detail.

SANDY (*delighted, muttering to herself*). 'Bumhole'!

RICHARD. Only a couple of months after we'd broken up.

BELLA. I did not! Alright, what did I say?

RICHARD. You said it was furrier than anyone else's.

EMILY. Oh, I remember him. 'Furry Jack.'

SANDY. 'Jack the Crack.'

RICHARD. It's just I hate the way that you women reduce sex in this way. You *reduce* it. You reduce it to the banal. You reduce it to . . . 'Bumhole'.

Some sniggers which he ignores.

No, I could do that if I wanted. Of course I could. I could . . . go around broadcasting those sort of details. But I choose not to. It ruins everything. Where can *love* fit in with that? Romance?

BELLA. Oh God . . . love . . . romance . . .

SANDY. Nonsense, Richard. You couldn't describe those sort of details.

RICHARD. I *could*, I just don't want to.

SANDY. You couldn't because you're not observant enough. You actually *dislike* looking at what's in front of you. You try to turn it into something else. Love. Romance. Bollocks. I mean, the perfect example was when you were painting your flat.

RICHARD. What are you talking about?

SANDY. You said it was called 'Parchment'. I saw it Richard. It was fucking *yellow*.

RICHARD. That's not me. That's Dulux for crying out loud.

60

SANDY. And it's exactly the same problem with your writing. You don't notice what's around you because you're not interested in it. You're only interested in yourself.

RICHARD. Crap. Complete crap.

TOM. Aren't writers meant to be interested in themselves?

SANDY (*ignoring him, to* RICHARD). Name me one intimate distinguishing feature of the last girl you slept with.

RICHARD. No.

SANDY. You see – you can't.

RICHARD. I can.

TOM. Maybe he doesn't want to.

SANDY. He can't. He probably had his eyes shut.

BELLA. He was probably busy looking at himself in the mirror.

TOM. Leave him alone.

BELLA. Don't take sides.

RICHARD. I fucking *can*, I just don't want to.

BELLA. Why not?

RICHARD. Because it would be a betrayal.

BELLA. We don't know who the girl is, Richard, how could it be a betrayal?

SANDY. Stop behaving like you're in court.

RICHARD. It's the principle of the thing.

BELLA (*to* SANDY). You're right. He can't.

RICHARD (*stung*). Fuck you.

Alright.

I noticed that she had extremely small nipples in proportion to the size of her breasts. Which were big. Nipples like a man. Almost like she didn't have any nipples at all. Very odd. And slightly off-putting.

Beat.

SANDY (*slightly taken aback*). Well done, Richard. You've proved me wrong. A moment of honesty.

Beat.

Yuk!

BELLA. Euuw. I think a breast without a nipple . . . is like a bum without a hole.

SANDY. I quite agree.

RICHARD. My point *is*, I wouldn't have *chosen* to share that detail with four other people. I mean, Tom, what do you feel about this? Give me some help here.

TOM. Well –

SANDY. Honesty is what –

RICHARD. Let the man *speak*!

SANDY *claps her hands over her mouth in mock humility.*

TOM. Well . . . I only see it from the man's point of view, obviously, but I think Richard's right. I don't like discussing – with other men – the . . . details of the girl I might be with, at the time. I think it's true. Men don't. Or if they do, they keep it vague. And . . . I think that's because . . . we don't want . . . to *share* . . . the girl . . . with anyone else.

Beat.

We don't want to give other men something to wank over.

We're not enlightened. It's a caveman thing. We want to boast . . . but we don't want to share. Not with other men. That belongs to us. Just us.

That's what it is. I think men – cavemen – are romantic.

Beat.

EMILY. That's lovely.

RICHARD. I agree. That's it. We don't want to share.

TOM. And it's not just that. When you think about what it's *like* . . . sex . . .

Beat.

You feel ashamed to talk about how it really is. Because if you *really* talked about what it was like, if you *really* shared what happened . . . It's . . .

. . . Incompetent . . . and it's . . . it's . . .

It's easier not to.

RICHARD. Yeah. So we don't.

Beat.

But you lot – (SANDY *and* BELLA.) – fucking *free*-for-all –

SANDY. Oh for Christ's sake, Richard, why are you taking it all so seriously? What's wrong with describing someone's cock? Or bumhole? It's a celebration. God is in the detail.

RICHARD. Because it objectifies. Well, I won't be objectified. I don't want to be a sex object.

SANDY. Don't you worry about that.

RICHARD. That's it. You *trivialise*. That's what you lot do. You trivialise sex. Well, sex isn't trivial. It's important. It's . . . potent.

BELLA. Richard, we know it's potent. Sex is the one area where we've got anything like the same amount of power as men –

SANDY. – if not more –

BELLA. – and we're damn well going to use it –

SANDY. – unlike any other field you care to mention –

BELLA. – and you don't *like* us using it because we're not necessarily going to use it to make you feel / comfortable.

RICHARD. / Oh, don't let's start on this one. *Everyone* knows women are much more powerful than men. Oppression, oppression, blah blah blah. No. It's *men* who are being oppressed. By chauvinist women. Look at you. You're oppressing me right now, you bitches.

SANDY. / We are not.

BELLA. / Bollocks, bollocks bollocksbollocks.

RICHARD. Tom. Give me some support here. Against them.

SANDY. You're wrong, you're wrong, you're wrong.

RICHARD. Take law.

Take law. Who –

BELLA *puts her hand over his mouth.* SANDY *puts her hands over her ears. He struggles to free himself.*

SANDY. La la la.

BELLA. Not listening, not listening –

RICHARD. Who –

EMILY. Bella – Sandy –

RICHARD. Who –

Who –

I will speak!

He frees himself by standing up and bangs on the table.

BELLA. Look at him, he can't *wait* to be a judge, can he.

SANDY. And get the *long* wig. The wig with the extensions.

RICHARD. Lawyers. Who are the most ambitious, aggressive, ruthless, high-flying lawyers? Let me tell you. The women.

BELLA. And why shouldn't they be?

SANDY. What do you want? You want them to be *caring*? You want them all to be fucking *nurses* and *teachers*? What's wrong with ambition? What's wrong with ruthlessness?

RICHARD. You *reward*, you reward qualities in women which you would punish in men! Sexual fundamentalism! Hotline to God! Everything's justified. Total subjectivity reigns. *I'm* not the one who's idealising women. *You* are. Sisterhood – bollocks. I mean, look at *her* – (SANDY.) Brainwashing you. Bullying you. Flirting with your ex (TOM.) half an hour ago –

SANDY. / Hang on –

RICHARD. / Female solidarity – suck my cock.

Beat.

SANDY. This is all very vague, Richard.

BELLA. And strangely self-righteous.

SANDY. And who's this 'you' that you keep talking about? Seems to me you're generalising just a bit here.

RICHARD. You're telling me you're not self-righteous? And that you never generalise?

64

SANDY. No. No we don't.

RICHARD. What do you mean, 'we'? Who is this 'we' you keep talking about, Ca-*ssandra*? Seems to me you're generalising just a bit here.

Beat.

BELLA. What's your problem, Richard?

RICHARD. My problem is with this fucking *narcissism*. Going *on* about the fact that you're women! You want to be treated as equal, why don't you shut up about it?

Beat.

TOM. I think the problem here –

SANDY (*to* RICHARD). Fuck you.

Beat.

EMILY. Why don't we all –

RICHARD. Oh, finally hit a nerve.

TOM. The problem with generalising –

BELLA. No, I resent this. You're including – you're confusing – me and Sandy with something that we're absolutely not, with those smug self-righteous careerist women –

SANDY. – Those women who endlessly *trade* on the fact that they're women –

BELLA. – And don't talk about anything else.

RICHARD. Look who's generalising now.

TOM. No wait, wait, wait. Hold on a minute.

SANDY. That journalist. Mary Tobias. Perfect example. Can't get *away* from her.

EMILY. Oh come on, she's alright.

BELLA. She's not alright, she's a boring talentless cunt, Emily. And a phoney. I went to school with her. Dimmest girl in the class. I remember. Even when we were little things making pictures out of dried pasta and Pritt Stick. Nothing's changed. Only now she's writing pieces. Pasta and Pritt Stick pieces. The prick. I'm fed up with hearing about her.

Beat.

Anyway, I digress.

Beat.

RICHARD. Wonderful.

Beat.

BELLA. That's right, that's right, that's where we were. You were saying women weren't oppressed. Bullshit.

RICHARD. No – 'Over-promoted' might be a more accurate description, from what I've just heard –

BELLA. Right. OK, Emily. How many female surgeons do you know?

EMILY. One.

BELLA. 'Nuff said.

RICHARD. How old is she? I bet you it's generational.

EMILY. Forty-five. Richard's right, there's already a younger generation coming through. Things are changing. I mean, *I'm* learning basic surgery. OK, the surgeon who teaches me is a bloke, but –

BELLA. You do surgery?!

RICHARD. I rest my case.

BELLA. But, you're, you can't do surgery! I mean –

SANDY. Do you practice on corpses?

EMILY. No. You learn on living bodies. I only do really basic stuff. I sort of . . . while he's cutting stuff – this surgeon – I hold stuff apart for him.

RICHARD. Stuff?

EMILY. Guts . . . that sort of thing. A lot of the time, I have my hands in people's guts. So that he can get at what he needs to. I kind of (*Gestures.*) hold them apart. For him.

Anyone at the table who is eating, slowly lets their fork fall.

Thank God. It's all gone quiet again.

TOM. What's . . . it like?

66

EMILY. It's fun. You get used to it very quickly.

TOM. Fuck, that's amazing. So . . . you actually know what we all look like inside.

EMILY. Yes.

SANDY. See – I only have a text-book diagram in my head, when I try to imagine it.

Beat.

How big's my womb?

EMILY. Small. (*Clenches fist.*) About this big.

TOM. What's it like, cutting through flesh? Is it anything like this steak?

He holds up a forkful.

SANDY. And when he *does* talk, he's Jack the Ripper.

EMILY. Well – it's not *unlike* that – I mean, that's obviously been cooked, so . . .

RICHARD. And . . . you don't find it . . .

EMILY. Oh no. No. I mean, the grossest thing so far was probably breast reduction. I helped him with one of those the other day.

TOM. Why's that?

EMILY. Well, it's just that he – you have to completely detach the nipple – of course you sew it back on later – and then he has to scoop out all the stuff inside, and I had to hold it for him, while he was scooping, and she was going from a 34 H –

SANDY. H?!

EMILY. – to a 34 B so there was a lot of stuff I had to hold on to, and it's slimy, and it's got all these yellow blobs in it, of fat, and stuff . . .

Sorry, am I putting people off?

ALL. No, no.

EMILY. . . . Anyway, mostly, I enjoy surgery.

They look at her. She is happily eating her food.

BELLA. And you never felt at a disadvantage? As a woman? You weren't patronised? Made to feel inferior?

EMILY. Me? No, not at all.

She takes another mouthful. Beat. RICHARD *pushes his plate away from him.*

But I'm not really interested in being a surgeon. I'm interested in the brain, and stuff . . . neurology . . . it's very trendy right now.

RICHARD. Neurology. It's the new black.

EMILY. You get to find out all about the interesting stuff.

TOM. Like what? What interesting stuff? Sorry – I work in the city!

EMILY. Memory, for example. What decides what's going to be a memory?

BELLA. What *does* decide it?

EMILY. Well, they're still finding out. Basically, whenever something new happens, the neurones in your brain have a sort of electrical conversation with each other, and sometimes it's quite quick, and then it goes silent. But sometimes, it turns into this lasting imprint.

There's only a brief window to turn something into memory, before it's lost.

SANDY (*to* TOM). Great trainers. Where did you get them?

TOM (*to* EMILY). What about when you remember something – and it's wrong?

EMILY. That's because memory's *got* to be malleable.

RICHARD. Why?

EMILY. So you can update it and correct it with new info. Basically, the thing about memory is you've got to think of it in 3D.

My consultant said, imagine a room, like a storeroom full of old furniture. Or, not a storeroom, more like . . . Memory's a bit like a room full of tuning forks.

RICHARD. What *are* you talking about?

EMILY. Well, imagine if this room was full of tuning forks –

RICHARD. Oh, you mean if this room turned into a metaphor.

EMILY. Yeah, if the room turned into a metaphor, and Tom hit one of these metaphorical tuning forks, and it started vibrating, *that* would be like a memory becoming active, entering consciousness. But the interesting thing is, as Tom's tuning fork vibrates –

SANDY. Do I get to hit one?

EMILY. – Shut up – the vibrations from Tom's tuning fork would set vibrations off in all the other tuning forks that were on its frequency, close to it in the room.

RICHARD (*to* EMILY). Oh, you mean like associated memories and associated knowledge.

EMILY. Exactly!

The angels are tinkling, quietly.

What's the first thing you can remember?

Pause.

TOM. A brown bench. I don't know why.

EMILY. Exactly. That's a *relic* you've retained, probably, of some . . . plans, or goals as a child.

What's interesting is how it *persists* . . . You can still *see* the bench, right?

TOM. Yes I can.

EMILY. Yeah. Because it's still there, in the 'room'.

Beat.

BELLA. Is it the chemicals?

EMILY. No, it's not the chemicals, because they break down over a couple of hours. And it's not the original neurones, because they die. But *something* carries on.

Pause.

TOM. What?

EMILY. They don't know. That's what they haven't worked out yet.

Pause.

RICHARD. Have you had any deaths?

EMILY. Not yet. I have had a crash call. When someone has a heart attack and you have to (*Mimes giving electric shock.*) with the defibrillator. And you don't half shit yourself.

(*To* RICHARD.) I mean, that's not to say that I haven't seen dead people. I just haven't been *responsible* for any deaths yet. Thank God.

But it's around you all the time. Of course it is.

Beat.

The other day I got asked how long someone had left to live. First time.

Beat.

RICHARD. What did you say?

EMILY. All the clichés. You think you won't but that's what you do. Because no one tells you how to do it. So all the clichés come out.

BELLA. What clichés?

EMILY. 'It could be weeks, it could be days. It's impossible to tell.'

Beat.

(*To all.*) Whereas actually, you know, my house officer told me to go and check on this guy, and he said, (*Blasé.*) 'Yeah, and then that should be it, I shouldn't think he'll make it beyond (*Checking watch.*) six o'clock.'

Six o'clock. You run out of time. Time's up.

And the nurses. They're like 'And how's Mr Hooper?' 'Oh, he died, bless him.' 'Oh, did he? Ahh. And how was your weekend?'

That's what it's like. Finishing. Lives finish all the time. People get old and die. And people die.

She meets BELLA*'s eye.*

Pause. A change in temperature. The table is still.

FATHER *appears at a distance from* BELLA. *He is in the dressing gown of his first two scenes. During the course of the conversation he approaches her until he is standing behind her.* BELLA *speaks looking straight ahead of her.*

FATHER. Statistically it's the logical choice.

BELLA (*wearily*). Oh, statistically.

FATHER. I've talked it through with your mother and she agrees with me.

BELLA. I don't care if you've talked it through with Mum. *I* don't agree with you.

Beat.

I mean, do *I* count for anything in all of this? 'Statistically'?

FATHER. Yes.

Beat.

Yes, you do. I want to know it's OK with you.

BELLA. But it's not! It's not OK with me, Dad. You know it's not.

Beat.

FATHER. But it's *my choice*.

BELLA. Yes, I knew that was coming. It's *your* choice.

Beat.

FATHER. You're not very forgiving, are you.

BELLA. Neither are you. Remember?

Pause.

Listen, don't pretend you need my blessing.

Nothing I say is going to make any difference to you.

You're going to do what you're going to do.

Because that's what you always do.

FATHER. It's not going to make any difference *what* I do. It's so aggressive. It's so fast-growing. And they can't *get* at it. Whatever I do, *it's not going to make any difference*.

I'm clear about this.

BELLA. I don't think you are.

Beat.

I don't think you are clear.

Sometimes, you're clear. Often, you're confused.

Beat.

You . . .

You said I was wearing school uniform the other day.

FATHER. You were wearing school uniform.

BELLA. I wasn't, I'd come from work. I'm grown up.

I'm not at school any more, Dad.

FATHER. Well, you should be.

Pause.

BELLA. Dad . . . listen to me . . . This is it . . . It's like . . .
You suddenly come into focus . . . then you're out of it
again . . . distant . . . emotionless . . . *carefree* . . . You're
there . . . then you're not . . . I don't know what to do . . .

I don't know what to do . . .

I don't know which is which any more.

Pause.

FATHER. Then you're the one who's confused.

*Beat. He is now standing behind her. He puts his hand on
her temple. Beat.*

(*Gently.*) This is the brain. The frontal lobes of the brain are
concerned with love, emotion, behaviour, memory . . .
romance . . .

Beat.

It's all going on in there.

*He takes his hand away, takes her hand and puts it on his
temple. Beat.*

There's something growing in there and there's no room for
it to grow.

She takes her hand away.

72

BELLA. Please.

You've got nothing to lose.

FATHER. My point exactly.

He disappears. The lights warm the rest of the table, gradually.

Pause.

RICHARD. Sobering thought.

SANDY. What?

RICHARD. Well, death.

Silence. The tinkling of the angels.

(*To* BELLA.) Do you think you'll ever get married?

Bella?

Pause.

BELLA. What?

RICHARD. Do you?

Beat.

BELLA. After seeing the way my father treated my mother? Christ, no. What's in it for me?

RICHARD. How did he treat your mother?

BELLA. You know how he treated my mother. Like shit.

RICHARD. When?

BELLA. When he fucked 'X'. When he fucked 'Y'. When he fucked whoever he wanted to fuck.

Beat.

RICHARD. Who thinks they'll get married? In the end? Hands up.

RICHARD, TOM, *and* EMILY *put up their hands.* SANDY *and* BELLA *do not.*

He leans back. Beat.

BELLA. What?

RICHARD. No, it's just . . . what I expected.

He idly scratches a scratchcard.

We still believe in love. You've decided not to.

BELLA. Back to love, again! Why are we talking about love? I thought we were talking about death.

Beat.

RICHARD. They're not unconnected.

Pause.

BELLA. I don't want to get married because I don't see what's in it for me.

RICHARD. But that's it. Marriage isn't about 'me'.

BELLA. And is that why yours didn't work?

Beat.

RICHARD. I wanted to marry you for a long time.

They look at each other. A pause. RICHARD *turns to* TOM.

Have you ever suffered from sexual jealousy, Tom?

TOM. Yes.

Beat.

A very unpleasant experience.

RICHARD. When did you last feel it?

TOM. Little while ago.

RICHARD. How would you describe it?

TOM. I don't know. You're the writer, mate.

SANDY. That's why he's asking you.

TOM. No it isn't.

RICHARD. Try and describe it.

Beat.

TOM. No.

RICHARD. Why not?

TOM. Because I don't want to talk about it.

RICHARD. Why not?

TOM. Because I don't need to.

RICHARD. *Need* to?

TOM. Yes. I don't *need* to talk about it.

RICHARD. Why not?

TOM. Because it's over. It's over, and I'm not angry about it any more, and I don't need to talk about it.

Beat.

RICHARD. Yes, you are.

TOM. No, I'm not.

Beat.

I'm not angry. You're the one who's angry.

Beat.

I know exactly what you're feeling. Because I felt it too.

Sexual jealousy's pornographic. You don't have the details. But you supply them.

It's about sitting there and thinking, he put that bit into that hole. Physical facts. (*He gestures to his head.*) Facts in your head.

RICHARD. He works in the city.

TOM. That's what you're thinking. I know that's what you're thinking because that's what I thought. Getting into my car very early one morning.

Beat.

In the end it goes away.

RICHARD. Does it?

Pause.

BELLA (*to* RICHARD). You were unfaithful too.

RICHARD. Only after you told me to be.

Beat.

BELLA (*to* RICHARD). Why did you have to bring all this up?

RICHARD. Why do you only ever see things from your point of view?

Why do you never try to see things from anyone else's perspective?

Why don't you care any more?

Beat.

BELLA. You know who you remind me of?

Beat.

You remind me of my father.

RICHARD. No. You know who's like your father?

You are.

BELLA. I am not.

RICHARD. You *are*. Both of you are always convinced you're right.

Beat.

And that everyone else is wrong.

BELLA. You're wrong.

RICHARD. See!

EMILY. Stop it. Make it up.

Beat.

BELLA. Richard, you don't really know my father.

RICHARD. I know you stopped speaking to him.

BELLA. Do you know *why* my father always thinks he's right? And that I'm wrong?

RICHARD. Because he's your father?

BELLA. No. Because I'm a woman and he's a man. Deep down, privately, he doesn't think women are as good as men. Nearly as good, but not quite.

That's why he reminds me of you.

So my mother will *never* be as important as him . . .

And my father thinks – he loves me very much, he loves us all very much – but deep down he thinks – my brothers are the talented ones. The clever ones.

They're the ones he's proud of.

Not me.

RICHARD. Not true.

BELLA. It is true.

Beat.

And it makes me feel competitive. Angry and competitive. I think, you're wrong. That's my reaction. You're wrong and I'm going to prove you wrong. I'll be tougher, and harder, and better. Because I'm right. Women can be better.

(*To* RICHARD.) I did see it from your perspective, Richard.

I felt what you felt. Jealousy.

But I think it comes with love. And I decided not to be in love. I didn't want to feel it. I decided to be hard.

Like you said.

And I know I ruined it.

And I'm sorry.

Beat.

I felt it with you. (TOM.)

Beat.

And it felt – it didn't feel like I thought it would.

Because it felt – more than anything else, in the end, it felt – competitive.

Competitive and angry.

I thought, you're not going to treat me like shit. I'm going to treat you like shit. First.

I ruined it when I tried not to care. And I ruined it when I did.

Beat.

TOM. Competitive . . .

BELLA. Competitive.

TOM. It's not a competition.

BELLA. I know. But it felt like it was. And I lost.

(*To* RICHARD.) And you think that makes me into a person who doesn't believe in love. You think I've decided to be a selfish, domineering, hard person.

And I think you're a selfish, domineering, sentimental person.

I annoy you. And you annoy me.

But you're right. I am deliberately hard, domineering, and selfish. And you know why? Because I saw my mother wasting her whole life on other people. Mainly my father. And I don't want to do that.

Beat.

And last night I couldn't get to sleep until three in the morning because my head was full of the people I've neglected.

Beat.

SANDY. Who have you neglected?

Beat.

BELLA. And it isn't going to be worth it. It isn't worth trying to be a success. Because it's not going to work.

Beat.

Why did my dad try and teach me Latin?

Beat.

See, I don't always think I'm right. That's where you're wrong, Richard: Wrong, wrong, wrong.

RICHARD. What?

Beat.

BELLA. Where are the great women?

Last night I realised – all my favourite authors are men.

Why aren't any of my favourite authors women?

Beat.

And it's not just writers. Composers. Conductors. Artists. I just don't think they're as good as the men. I don't think women are as good as men.

SANDY. No.

BELLA. So there you are, Richard.

SANDY. Bella, this is . . .

Beat.

How can you say that? What about . . . what about . . .

RICHARD. George Eliot.

BELLA. She's dead. Doesn't count.

RICHARD. Why not?

BELLA. Because that's . . . that's cherry-picking. It doesn't
mean anything. I'm talking about at any one time. Look at
the proportions at any one time. I'm talking about now.
Now. Weigh up the men and weigh up the women. Who are
the great women now?

Beat.

SANDY. This is –

BELLA. I don't know if I even like women. If I'm honest . . .
I think I've got a prejudice against them.

SANDY. Where's all this come from?

Beat.

Of course you – I mean – what about us.

Beat.

BELLA. Well, Emily doesn't count, because she's a doctor and
that's good and she's my oldest friend.

SANDY. What about me?

BELLA. You're not a woman, you're a man.

Beat.

RICHARD. I'm not listening to this. It's ridiculous.

BELLA. But I bet, deep down, you agree.

SANDY. I'm not listening either, Bella. Think about what
you've just said. No, *think* about it. And it'll turn into . . .
loo paper in your hands.

Beat.

All of this is just because you're upset with Richard.

Beat.

Of course you like women. And of course there are talented women. You're just insecure. Because you're a woman. We're all insecure. I look at my writing and I think, yes, second-rate Will Self.

RICHARD. Will Self *is* second-rate.

SANDY. Shut up, Richard. It's genetic. Women are more prone to insecurity than men. Men have this wonderful arrogance. They don't *question* anything. They don't question themselves.

RICHARD. We fucking do! If you think that, you're even more stupid than I thought.

SANDY. Shut up, Richard.

RICHARD. I will not shut up. I'm fed up with this. You're one of the most arrogant people I've ever met. And I've never once known you 'question' yourself.

SANDY. I do. I do question myself. Of course I do.

RICHARD. Oh yeah.

SANDY. I do. Take my writing.

RICHARD. What about your writing?

Beat.

SANDY. I can't write anything deep.

Beat.

BELLA. Sandy. You always get like this after two drinks.

SANDY. No, it's true.

You need light and you need dark. And I can't do it.

And it shakes me up when you say you don't think women have got it in them. I don't ever want to hear you say that again. You don't say that stuff.

BELLA. Why not?

SANDY (*forcefully*). Because there are people who are *waiting* to agree with you.

Beat. She fingers the lawyer's wig.

(*Matter-of-fact.*) There's nothing like feeling like you can't write.

You know what it feels like?

You feel ashamed.

Because you're just pretending.

Pause. RICHARD *takes the wig from her.*

RICHARD. Everyone starts by pretending. If you can't do it, you can't do it. But you have to start by pretending that you can. With everything. Then you find out if you're right.

Beat.

BELLA. I didn't start by pretending. When I was little . . . I didn't need to pretend . . . because I was special.

And I'm not special any more.

SANDY. Of course you're special.

BELLA. I'm not. I'm not any more. It's gone.

Pause.

RICHARD. You're twenty-nine. You're a different person. You don't know if you were special or not. What does that *mean*?

BELLA. It was special.

RICHARD. Everything looks special in retrospect.

Beat.

BELLA. Don't you remember what it was like?

Beat.

RICHARD. It's all photos.

BELLA. What do you mean?

RICHARD. It always turns out what I'm remembering is a photo.

BELLA. I'm not talking about a photo.

Beat.

Doesn't anyone know what I'm talking about?

Things my dad used to say.

He used to read me Dickens.

I'm twenty-nine.

I'm never going to be twenty-eight again.

I'm never going to be eight again.

And I miss it.

I've left so much behind.

And it all gets lost.

Pause.

I can remember my mother holding me up in front of the mirror. Saying 'Who's that? Who's that?'

I can see her, see her face. But I can't see me. My reflection in the mirror.

Pause.

(*To* RICHARD.) Remember when we met.

Beat.

RICHARD. I remember.

BELLA. What do you remember?

Beat.

RICHARD. I can't make you understand it.

Beat.

BELLA. You should be with her. (EMILY.)

You like her. She likes you.

I'm no good for you.

Pause.

RICHARD. Why can't you take love? Why won't you believe in it?

BELLA. I don't know.

I can't take a compliment.

RICHARD. Believe in it.

82

BELLA. I can't.

RICHARD. You can. It's all in your head.

BELLA. Where else would it be?

Pause.

RICHARD. Listen to me. Wake up. You know the truth about
your father? You're his favourite.

BELLA. No.

RICHARD. This bollocks about your brothers. You don't
understand. I can see it. He adores you.

BELLA. No. It's more complicated than that.

RICHARD. No it's not. Dots. Join the dots, Bella. Why can't
you see it?

Beat.

It's not complicated. It's unconditional. Take it.

BELLA. It is complicated. There *are* conditions.

RICHARD. No there aren't.

BELLA. There are always conditions. Love is full of
conditions. Only if you do what I tell you. Only if you do
what I say. Only if you're a success.

My relationship with my father was good.

My relationship with my father was bad.

It was the best of times, it was the worst of times, it was the
spring of hope, it was the winter of despair.

I can't make you understand it. There isn't a broad sketch.

It's all perspective.

Beat.

He's in hospital. He's in hospital and he's dying. He's not
going to be around much longer.

Pause.

RICHARD. Christ, I'm sorry.

Pause.

SANDY. What's he dying of?

BELLA. We thought it was a stroke. He was forgetting words. He was seeing things. We got it wrong. It turned out he had cancer. The tumour was pressing on the optic nerve. It's the size of an apple. He's on his way out. (*To* EMILY.) Days, not weeks.

It could be any time. It could be tonight.

Pause.

Now is when I really need my dad.

Because my dad is dying.

What am I going to do without him telling me what to do?

Silence.

SANDY. Bella. I'm sorry.

RICHARD. I'm so sorry.

SANDY. Bella.

How . . .

How are you feeling?

Pause.

BELLA. I'm feeling all the clichés.

Beat.

'His heart was heavy.' Do you know how right that is?

It *is* heavy. I can feel it here.

Pause.

I feel it when I'm lying in bed and I can't sleep. I lie in bed and I listen to my watch ticking . . .

I'm losing someone.

BELLA *is crying.*

. . . I'm sorry . . .

. . . I'm sorry . . .

I don't know what to do.

SANDY. Sweetheart . . . You shouldn't be with us. Go and be with him. Before it's too late.

EMILY *gets up*.

EMILY. Bella. It's OK.

BELLA *gets up*.

BELLA. I'm sorry . . .

TOM. Shall I . . . go and ask them to sort out a cab for her?

EMILY *nods.* TOM *gets up and goes off. They sit, frozenly.*
EMILY *hugs* BELLA. SANDY *hovers, touching* BELLA*'s*
shoulders. RICHARD *is excluded.*

RICHARD. It's OK.

Pause. Somewhere, a phone rings.

Oh God.

He finds his phone, switches it off. Stands. TOM *comes*
back in.

TOM (*in an undertone*). I've asked them to get her a cab.

RICHARD. Great.

TOM. Who's going to go with her?

RICHARD. What?

TOM. Who's going to go with her?

RICHARD. Where?

TOM. To the hospital.

Beat.

RICHARD. I'll go with her.

The embrace dissolves.

Bella.

Do you want me to go with you?

Beat.

BELLA. No.

RICHARD. You sure?

BELLA. Yes.

She leaves. Slowly, the rest sit down. No one knows what to
say. Pause. They look at the candles.

SANDY. I can't tell which way they're going round.

Beat.

TOM (*quietly*). Clockwise.

EMILY. Anticlockwise.

RICHARD. No, clockwise.

The lights come down until the stage is only lit by the candles and the shadows of the turning angels are thrown up against the wall. Very quietly, their tinkling noise, and in the distance, the noises of the restaurant.

SANDY *leans forward slowly, and blows the candles out. Blackout on the table.*

Lights up on BELLA's FATHER. *In the dressing gown.*

FATHER. No.

Where?

Over here?

No.

He moves a little to look into the room

There?

In the curtain?

No.

No. I can't see it.

Listen, Rabbit, it's a curtain. Nothing there.

He listens a moment.

I *am* looking at it.

Bella –

OK, OK.

He walks over to inspect something.

OK, I'm looking right at it and there's nothing there.

It's a curtain. Simple. See?

No face.

No face. It's just the wrinkles in the cloth. Nothing there.

86

Nothing to worry about.

Well . . .

Think about tomorrow. Think about tomorrow morning.

He walks back to the door.

Do you want the door open or shut?

OK. I'll leave the light on outside.

OK now?

See you in the morning.

Night, sweetheart.

Night night.

Blackout.

The End.